PENGUINS

Photo credits:

Tom & Pat Leeson—Cover, Page 19-20, 22-23, 26-29, 31
Francois Gohier—Pages 4-10, 20-21, 24-25
Kjell B. Sandved/Visuals Unlimited—Pages 5-9, 15-17, 23, 30
John Gerlach/Visuals Unlimited—Page 9, 18
Don W. Fawcett/Visuals Unlimited—Page 11
Brian Rogers/Visuals Unlimited—Pages 12-13
John Eastcott/Yva Momatiuk/DRK Photo—Page 8
Dennis Frieborn/Wildlife Collection—Page 8
H. Rappl/Wildlife Collection—Page 14
Chris Huss/Wildlife Collection—Page 25
Robin Makowski—Page 13

ISBN: 0-590-96962-5

12 11 10 9 8 7 6 5 4 3 2   7 8 9/9 0/0

Printed in the U.S.A.   23

First Scholastic printing, January 1997

PENGUINS

By Stacy Savran

Scholastic Inc.
New York   Toronto   London   Auckland   Sydney

What Is a Penguin?

Penguins waddle when they walk. They swim, but they can't fly. The first people who saw penguins called them "feathered fish." But in fact, penguins are seabirds.

Feathered Friends

There are 17 different kinds of penguins. They all live in the southern half of the world. Some live in freezing cold

Antarctica and others in warmer places.
Penguins spend a lot of time at sea.
When they come ashore they form large
groups, or *colonies*.

Look-alikes

How can you tell penguins apart? Each kind has a special pattern in its feathers. Penguins also come in different sizes. The Emperor is the biggest. The Little Penguin is the smallest.

Emperor penguin

Little penguin

Rockhopper penguin

How can a penguin family find each other in a crowd? Each penguin sings its own special song.

Chinstrap penguin

Macaroni penguin

Magellanic penguin

Gentoo penguin

King penguin family

Coming Ashore

Penguins come on land to shed old feathers and grow new ones. This is called *molting.*

They also come ashore to have babies. Some penguins build nests. The Magellanic penguin makes a nest by digging a deep hole with its feet and bill. King and Emperor penguins do not make nests at all.

Egg-sitting

A penguin egg is about the size of a grapefruit. Parents take turns sitting on it.

Emperor penguins lay eggs during the winter. Only the male is big enough to keep the egg warm. He balances it on his feet for two months. He doesn't even stop to eat!

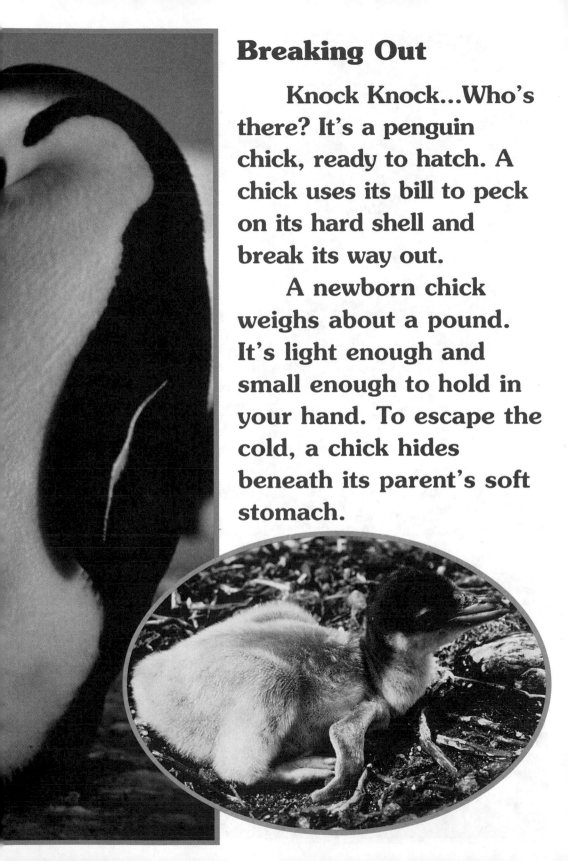

Breaking Out

Knock Knock...Who's there? It's a penguin chick, ready to hatch. A chick uses its bill to peck on its hard shell and break its way out.

A newborn chick weighs about a pound. It's light enough and small enough to hold in your hand. To escape the cold, a chick hides beneath its parent's soft stomach.

Munch a Mouthful

Hungry chicks must wait for their parents to bring them food. The chicks are still too young to head for the sea. An adult penguin stores food in its mouth. The chick uses its bill to reach in and grab a mouthful.

On Their Own

When chicks have plumped up, they no longer need their parents for warmth and protection. Some chicks join together to form a nursery. They squeeze side-by-side for warmth and safety.

Chick Change

As chicks grow they begin to lose their fuzzy gray or brown feathers. Thick layers of black and white feathers take their place.

Wearing their new coat, chicks head to the sea for the first time. This is called *fledging*.

King penguins waddling

Getting Around

To get around on land, penguins waddle, hop, or run. On soft snow or sand, a penguin can glide on its belly. It uses its feet to push along. This is called *tobogganing*.

Rockhopper penguins bounce over rocks and cliffs with both feet held together. Unlike penguins that dive into the water, rockhoppers jump in feet first!

Adélie penguin
tobogganing

Rockhopper penguins jumping

Super Swimmers

Penguins are graceful swimmers. They "fly" through the water, flapping their flippers like wings.

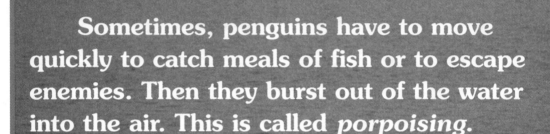

Sometimes, penguins have to move quickly to catch meals of fish or to escape enemies. Then they burst out of the water into the air. This is called *porpoising.*

Peguin Talk

Penguins speak their own language with their bill and their body.

When penguins find mates, they stand face-to-face with their bills stretched up to the sky and their wings back. Then they bow to each other and sing special songs.

Teamwork

Living where it's cold is hard work. Penguins must cooperate to keep warm. Some huddle together and keep shuffling around. That way, each penguin can make its way to the warm center of the group.

Did You Know?

• • Penguins make a lot of noise. Their chatter is called *trumpeting*.

• • The largest penguin colony in the world has over 600,000 penguins in it!

• • Many penguins are not afraid of people and like to follow them around!